I Wonder Why

There's a Hole In The Sky

and Other Questions About The Environment

Sean Callery

KINGFISHER

NEW YORK

Text copyright © 2008 by Kingfisher
KINGFISHER
Published in the United States by Kingfisher, an imprint
of Henry Holt and Company LLC, 175 Fifth Avenue, New
York, New York 10010. First published in Great Britain by
Kingfisher Publications plc, an imprint of Macmillan's
Children's Books, London.

Distributed in Canada by H. B. Fenn and Company Ltd.

Library of Congress Cataloging-in-Publication Data
Callery, Sean.
   I wonder why there's a hole in the sky and other
questions about the environment/Sean Callery.
      p. cm.
   Includes index.
   1. Environmental sciences—Juvenile literature.
   2. Environmental protection—Juvenile literature.
   3. Nature—Effect of human beings on—Juvenile
literature. I. Title.
   GE115.C35 2008
   363.7—dc22   2007045648

ISBN 978-0-7534-6249-2

Kingfisher books are available for special promotions
and premiums. For details contact: Director of Special
Markets, Holtzbrinck Publishers.

First American Hardback Edition July 2008
Printed in Taiwan
10 9 8 7 6 5 4 3 2 1

1TR/0108/SHENS/RNBW(RNBW)/126.6MA/F

Illustrations: Mark Bergin 25, 30–31; Martin Camm
18–19; Peter Dennis (Linda Rogers Agency) 10, 12,
14–15, 26–27, 28; Chris Forsey cover, 16; Linden Artists 3,
9, 21, 22, 29; Julian Baker title page, 6, 8, 10–11, 30–31;
Peter Wilks (SGA) all cartoons.

CONTENTS

4 Why is there life on Earth?

5 How can a star keep us warm?

5 What is the weather?

6 Which blanket keeps Earth warm?

7 How is the atmosphere like a greenhouse?

7 What are greenhouse gases?

8 Why are trees the "bee's knees?"

8 How does water cycle?

9 Why can't we chop until we drop?

10 What makes gas?

10 Why is farming such a gas?

11 What's that smell?

12 Is it me, or is it hot here?

12 Is this a wind-up?

13 Has our climate always changed?

14 Are we up to our necks in floods?

15 What's wrong with parking lots?

15 Who turned off the rain?

16 Why are the poles hot stuff?

17 Why is ice so cool?

17 When is a river not a river?

18 Why is there a hole
  in the sky?

19 Is the hole in the sky
  always there?

20 How can water be
  bad for you?

20 When is oil like glue?

21 What air makes you choke?

22 Why are some animals
  on the move?

22 Who needs a place
  to call home?

23 Who is a tiger's
  worst enemy?

24 What energy
  never runs out?

24 How can the Sun light
  up our nights?

25 How is wind farmed?

26 Why say bye
  to flying?

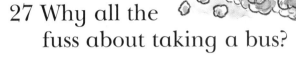

26 What are
  food miles?

27 Why all the
  fuss about taking a bus?

28 Why is garbage such a
  waste?

29 What are the three Rs?

29 When is a worm my friend?

30 How can I have a greener
  house?

30 When is "off" not "off"?

31 Why are some light
  bulbs greedy?

31 How else can
  I save energy?

32 Index

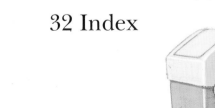

Why is there life on Earth?

There is life on Earth because it is not too hot and not too cold. We are exactly the right distance from the Sun, which gives us heat and light. This is why there is no life on our neighboring planets, Venus (too hot) or Mars (too cold).

Sun

Mercury

Venus

Earth

Mars

Jupiter

• Some experts call Earth the "Goldilocks planet" because, just like the porridge that Goldilocks eats in *Goldilocks and the Three Bears*, it is not too hot and not too cold.

How can a star keep us warm?

The Sun is a star, just like the ones that we see in the sky at night. It looks bigger than the other stars because it is much closer to us. The Sun's rays are very hot, and they warm Earth.

● It takes around eight minutes for the Sun's rays to reach Earth across space. They travel the 93 million miles at 1.1 billion miles per hour.

● Clouds are made up of tiny drops of water. These bump into each other and make larger drops. When they get too big, they fall to the ground as rain or snow.

What is the weather?

There are all types of weather. It can be sunny, cloudy, wet, snowy, windy, or stormy. Both the Sun's heat and changes in the air above Earth affect the weather. The usual weather of a region or country is called its climate.

Some types of weather

sunny

cloudy

heavy rain

thunder showers

snow

tropical storm

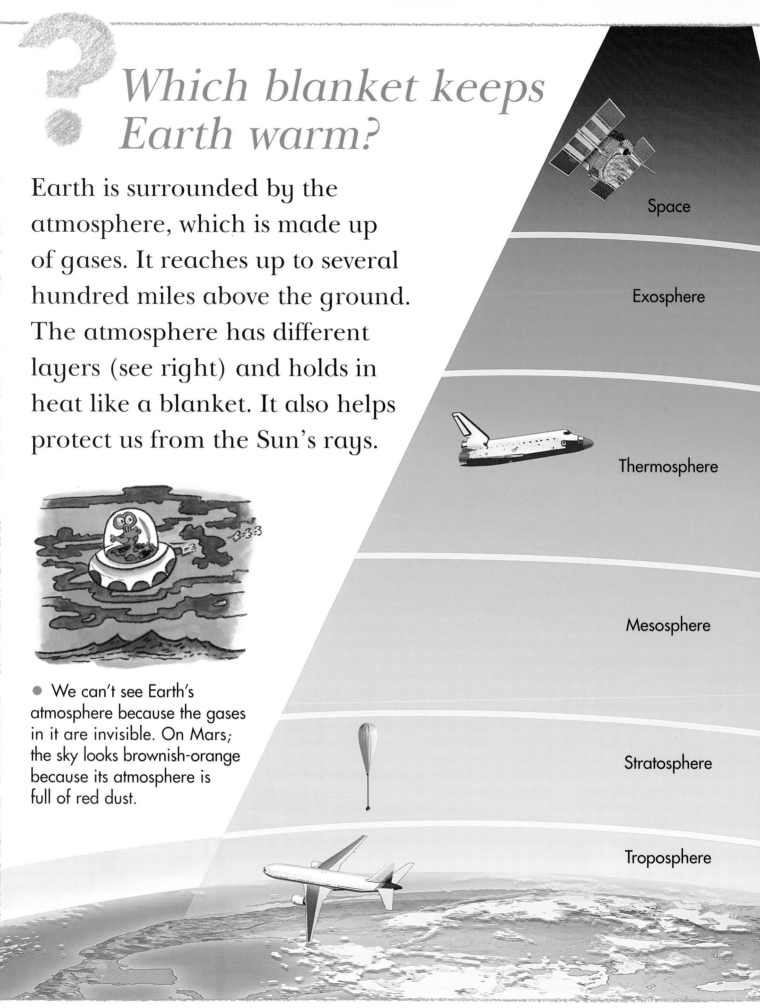

Which blanket keeps Earth warm?

Earth is surrounded by the atmosphere, which is made up of gases. It reaches up to several hundred miles above the ground. The atmosphere has different layers (see right) and holds in heat like a blanket. It also helps protect us from the Sun's rays.

● We can't see Earth's atmosphere because the gases in it are invisible. On Mars, the sky looks brownish-orange because its atmosphere is full of red dust.

Space

Exosphere

Thermosphere

Mesosphere

Stratosphere

Troposphere

How is the atmosphere like a greenhouse?

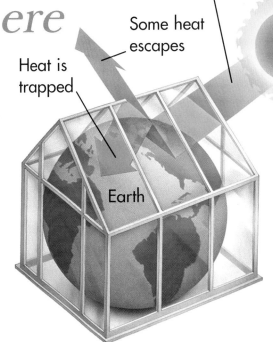

Sun's heat

Some heat escapes

Heat is trapped

Sun

Earth

It gets very warm in a greenhouse because the glass walls and roof stop the heat from escaping. Gases in our atmosphere trap heat in the same way and keep Earth warm. They are called greenhouse gases.

● The atmosphere on Venus may once have been like ours, but surface temperatures there are now around 860°F (460°C)—much, much hotter than your oven at its hottest.

What are greenhouse gases?

The main greenhouse gas is water vapor (water that has turned into a gas). Other greenhouse gases include carbon dioxide, methane, and nitrous oxide (see pages 10–11). Some of these gases can remain in Earth's atmosphere for more than 100 years.

● Greenhouse gases are made both naturally and by the things that people do. For example, both volcanoes and cars blast out carbon dioxide.

Why are trees the "bee's knees?"

Trees take carbon dioxide from the air and make oxygen—the gas that we need in order to breathe. Trees also store carbon in their wood. If there were no trees, there would be so much carbon dioxide in the air that we wouldn't be able to breathe.

● Rainforests are home to two thirds of all of the different types of animals and plants on Earth. In fact, thousands of them are only found in rainforests.

How does water cycle?

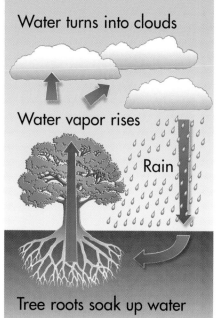

Water turns into clouds

Water vapor rises

Rain

Tree roots soak up water

Water moves in a cycle. Tree roots soak up water. The water moves to the leaves and enters the air as vapor. This vapor rises and turns into clouds. When it rains, the cycle starts again.

- If you plant a tree, it will store carbon all of its life. This will help cut greenhouse gases.

Why can't we chop until we drop?

Cutting down trees and burning them damages our planet. This is because there are fewer trees to make oxygen and the ground that is left behind is likely to flood. Burning wood also releases carbon dioxide into the atmosphere.

- Over the last 60 years, around half of the world's rainforests have been cut down. This is so that people can use the wood and the land.

What makes gas?

Carbon dioxide is given off by power plants burning coal, oil, and gas. A lot of carbon dioxide also comes from vehicles such as cars, trucks, and airplanes.

● Those pretty, wispy trails that airplanes leave behind in the sky are not good for the planet. They are made from water vapor and exhaust fumes containing carbon dioxide.

Why is farming such a gas?

Some farmers put fertilizers that make nitrous oxide onto their fields. Although there is not much of this gas in the atmosphere, it can hang around for 150 years. This is a problem because it traps heat.

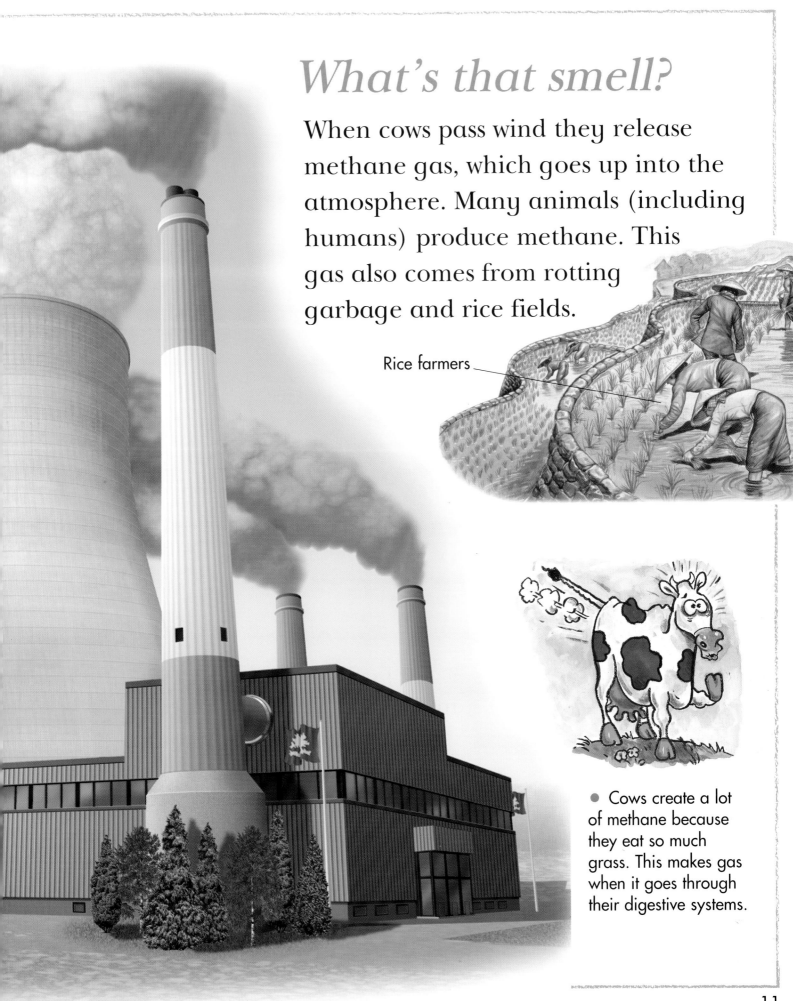

What's that smell?

When cows pass wind they release methane gas, which goes up into the atmosphere. Many animals (including humans) produce methane. This gas also comes from rotting garbage and rice fields.

Rice farmers

● Cows create a lot of methane because they eat so much grass. This makes gas when it goes through their digestive systems.

Is it me, or is it hot here?

All around the world, temperatures are rising. This is called global warming. In the summer of 2003, Europe got so hot that 35,000 people died and there were forest fires. The summer of 2005 broke high temperature records across the U.S.A.

● The snow cap that has been on the top of Mount Kilimanjaro, in Africa, for 11,000 years is melting. By 2015, it may have completely disappeared.

Is this a wind-up?

The world is seeing more extreme weather such as hurricanes, tornadoes, and typhoons. There are now twice as many big storms over the Atlantic Ocean as there were 100 years ago.

Has our climate always changed?

Earth has gone through several ice ages and different climates. For example, from 65 million years ago to 100 million years ago, the temperature was around 50°F (10°C) warmer, and dinosaurs lived in forests at the South Pole. But the climate has never changed as fast as it is changing right now.

● Woolly mammoths lived in Siberia more than 11,000 years ago. When temperatures rose by just a few degrees, it is possible that they couldn't stand the heat and died out.

Are we up to our necks in floods?

The world seems to be suffering from more floods. Between 2005 and 2007, in Australia, the U.S.A., India, the U.K., and eastern Europe, heavy rainfall caused landslides and made rivers burst their banks, flooding streets and houses.

● Scientists believe that 5 percent more rain, snow, and sleet is falling in the U.S.A. and Europe than 100 years ago.

14

What's wrong with parking lots?

Building roads and parking lots make floods more likely because water is unable to soak into the ground. Instead, it quickly runs off the top of these hard surfaces, causing problems.

• Lack of water is bad news, too. In 2007, there were major droughts in southern Europe. In Australia, a six-year-long drought, the worst on record, dried out rivers and caused water shortages.

Who turned off the rain?

There have also been more droughts recently. In a drought, not enough rain falls. There is very little drinking water, and it is difficult to grow crops. Since the 1970s, the number of serious droughts in the world has doubled.

Why are the poles hot stuff?

Earth spins around the North and South poles. The North Pole is in the Arctic, and the South Pole is in the Antarctic. Both poles are covered in ice, but rising temperatures are causing the ice to melt. Even a small rise in temperature can melt huge amounts of polar ice.

● Soon there will not be enough sea ice in the Arctic for polar bears to live on. They are already losing weight as their hunting grounds disappear.

Why is ice so cool?

Because ice is white, it reflects the Sun's rays and helps keep Earth cool. Icecaps are an important habitat (home) for animals such as polar bears and penguins.

● If the entire Greenland ice sheet melted in the Arctic, sea levels would rise by 23 feet (7m). Several coastal cities would be underwater, and entire low-lying countries, such as Bangladesh, would be destroyed.

When is a river not a river?

Glaciers are rivers of ice that move very slowly. They drain into streams that supply water to people farther down the river. Some glaciers are melting and getting smaller, so less water is reaching these people.

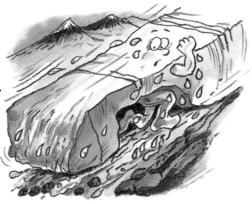

● The total surface area of the world's glaciers has shrunk by half in the last 100 years.

Why is there a hole in the sky?

High up in the atmosphere is the ozone layer. It filters out the Sun's harmful rays. The ozone layer is damaged by chemicals called chlorofluorocarbons (CFCs for short), which were used in aerosol (spray) cans and fridges. CFCs have made a big hole in the ozone layer over Antarctica.

Hole in the ozone layer

Antarctica

Is the hole in the sky always there?

No, the hole opens and closes as the seasons change. So far the biggest hole appeared over Antarctica in 2006. There is no hole above the Arctic, but the ozone has gotten thinner. CFCs have been used less since 1987, and the damage to the ozone layer has slowed down.

hydrochlorofluorocarbons

● CFCs have been replaced by hydrochlorofluorocarbons (or HCFCs) that are much less damaging, but even more difficult to spell!

● Jet airplanes fly in the ozone layer, between 6 and 25 miles (10 and 40km) above Earth's surface. Their engines release chemicals that damage the layer.

How can water be bad for you?

We need fresh water in order to live, but when chemicals and human waste get into rivers and lakes, water becomes polluted (dirty). This kills five million people per year—that's around 14,000 deaths per day, just from dirty water.

When is oil like glue?

When oil tankers leak, they cause incredible damage to the environment, especially to sea birds, seals, and sea otters. The oil sticks to their feathers or skin and makes it difficult for them to move or stay warm.

● In 1989, an oil tanker called *Exxon Valdez* spilled a lot of oil in Alaska, killing between 250,000 and 500,000 sea birds and 2,800 to 5,000 sea otters.

What air makes you choke?

Smoke from factories and fumes from engine exhaust pipes send dirt and gas into the air, making it difficult to breathe. In some cities, you can see the pollution hanging in the air. This is called smog.

● In 1952, smog over London, England, killed 12,000 people. The dense fog was called a "pea souper" because it was thick, like pea soup.

Why are some animals on the move?

Animals sense when the climate changes, and, as a result, some are moving to cooler regions. In North America, the red fox is moving into the Arctic and threatening the arctic fox, which cannot compete with its larger cousin.

Who needs a place to call home?

Elephants roam the grasslands of Africa and Asia. A lot of this land is being turned into farmland, so the elephants are losing their habitat. This means that elephants could become extinct (die out).

Who is a tiger's worst enemy?

For a long time, people have hunted tigers for their skins and body parts, which are then used in medicines. Hunting tigers is now against the law in most countries, but people still catch them illegally.

● Many American pikas, or rock rabbits, are moving to higher ground because they like cool temperatures. The warmer climate may make them extinct.

● The dodo was a flightless bird that lived in Mauritius. It became extinct more than 300 years ago when it was hunted to death.

What energy never runs out?

Energy from water, the wind, or the Sun is called renewable energy. Unlike oil, gas, or coal, it will never run out. Also, it does not produce carbon dioxide, so it will not speed up global warming.

● Scientists are trying to figure out how to make power from the movement of waves. So, in the future, our homes could run on wave power.

How can the Sun light up our nights?

Solar cells use the Sun's rays to make electricity. They can be used for lights outside or in roof panels to power entire houses. Solar collectors use the Sun's heat to warm water.

Solar panels

● If we covered the Sahara Desert with solar panels, it would make more electricity than the world could even use.

How is wind farmed?

People have used wind power for many years. The first wind-powered machines were windmills. Now, long blades spin in giant wind farms around the world. This type of farm can be built out at sea too.

● Some power plants have started to burn crops such as straw, willow, and elephant grass to make electricity.

Why say bye to flying?

Airplanes give off a huge amount of carbon dioxide. To travel in a "greener" way, take vacations closer to home instead of flying. If you have to fly, try to get a direct flight, because taking off and landing use up the most energy.

What are food miles?

If something you eat comes from another country, it traveled many "food miles" to get to you and a lot of carbon dioxide was produced on the way. Buying food that is grown locally is often better for the environment.

Why all the fuss about taking a bus?

Traveling by bus or train does less damage to the environment than going by car because a lot of people share the energy that is used.

- Cycling and walking are much better for the environment than using a car because they do not burn oil.

- If people share a car, they use less energy. Some roads have special lanes for cars carrying more than one person.

Why is garbage such a waste?

Most of our garbage is burned or buried in massive garbage dumps called landfill sites. Rain can wash poisons from the garbage into the soil and pollute the water supply. Landfill sites also release horrible gases into the air.

What are the three Rs?

Reduce, Reuse, and Recycle—we should reduce what we throw away, reuse things as much as possible, and when we don't need them anymore, recycle rather than throwing them out. As much as 70 percent of our garbage could be recycled.

● Recycling one aluminum can saves enough energy to run a TV for three hours.

When is a worm my friend?

Compost is an excellent way to reduce waste and help your garden. Put old leaves, plants, fruit and vegetable peelings, eggshells, and newspapers in a special container outside. Worms and insects will turn it into soil for the garden.

● Cut-up newspaper is perfect in a compost pile because it soaks up moisture. Then, tiny animals will munch away and break it up.

How can I have a greener home?

A "green" home might have solar panels, solar collectors, and a wind turbine on the roof (see pages 24–25). Insulation would be installed to keep in the heat. Outside, rainwater could be collected in a tank, and kitchen waste would be put into a compost pile.

● Turn down the heating by a couple of degrees to save energy and reduce your heating bills. You won't even notice the difference.

Solar panels

Solar collectors

Compost pile

When is "off" not "off"?

Appliances left on standby, instead of being turned off, use between 10 and 60 percent of the power that they use when they are on. Turn off your television, stereo, and computer monitor when you're not using them.

● In the U.K., the average household has 12 machines on standby at any one time. That's a lot of wasted energy.

Conservatory traps heat

Why are some light bulbs greedy?

Most of the energy that goes into standard light bulbs is changed into heat rather than light. Switching to low-energy light bulbs, which use less power than regular light bulbs, saves both energy and money.

Wind turbine

Rainwater tank

How else can I save energy?

Turn off lights when you can and try not to use too much hot water. When you take a shower or bath, or make a hot drink, use only as much water as you need.

Insulated walls

● One energy-saving light bulb uses up to one quarter of the electricity that ordinary light bulbs use, but it will last up to 12 times longer.

Index

A

airplanes 10, 19, 26
Antarctic 16, 18, 19
Arctic 16, 17, 19, 22
arctic foxes 22
atmosphere 6, 7, 9, 10, 11, 18

C

carbon dioxide 7, 8, 9,10,
  24, 26
cars 7, 10, 15, 27
CFCs 18–19
chemicals 19, 20
climate 5, 13, 22–23
clouds 5, 8
compost 29, 30
cows 11
cycling 27

D

dinosaurs 13
dodos 23
droughts 15

E

electricity 24–25, 31
elephants 22
energy 24–25, 26, 29, 30–31

F

factories 21
farmers 10–11
floods 9, 14–15
food miles 26
forest fires 12

G

garbage 28–29
gases 6–7, 8, 10–11, 21,
  24, 28
glaciers 17
global warming 12, 24
greenhouse gases 7, 9

H

habitats 17, 22
hurricanes 12

I

ice 16–17
ice ages 13
insulation 30–31

L

landfill sites 28
light bulbs 31

M

Mars 4, 6
methane 7, 11
Mount Kilimanjaro 12

N

nitrous oxide 7, 10
North Pole 16

O

oil 20, 24, 27
oxygen 8, 9
ozone layer 18–19

P

penguins 17
pikas 23
polar bears 16–17
poles 16–17
pollution 20–21
power plants 10, 25

R

rain 5, 14–15, 28
rainforests 8, 9
recycling 28–29
red foxes 22
roads 15

S

sea otters 20
sea birds 20
seals 20
smog 21
solar cells 24
solar collectors
  24, 30
solar panels 24, 30
South Pole 13, 16
Sun 4–5, 6, 17, 18, 24

T

tigers 23
tornadoes 12
travel 26–27
trees 8–9
typhoons 12

V

Venus 4, 7

W

water 7, 8, 15, 17, 20, 24
water cycle 8
wave power 24
weather 5, 12
wind 24–25
wind farms 25
wind turbines 30–31
windmills 25